# My Life As a Dog

## *The Many Moods of Lucy, the Dog of a Thousand Faces*

Geoff Hansen

**Andrews McMeel
Publishing**

Kansas City

www.andrewsmcmeel.com

99 00 01 02 03 TWP 10 9 8 7 6 5 4 3 2 1

Library of Congress Cataloging-in-Publication Data

Hansen, Geoff.
   My life as a dog : the many moods of Lucy, the dog of a thousand faces / Geoff Hansen
      p.   cm.
   ISBN 0-7407-0033-2 (hardcover)
   1. Beagle (Dog breed)--Vermont--Pictorial works.  2. Beagle (Dog breed)--Vermont--Anecdotes.  3. Photography of dogs.  I. Title.
SF429.B3H36  1999
636.753'7'0222--dc21                                                           99-18475
                                                                                CIP

*Design by Holly Camerlinck*

ATTENTION: SCHOOLS AND BUSINESSES

Andrews McMeel books are available at quantity discounts with bulk purchase for educational, business, or sales promotional use. For information, please write to: Special Sales Department, Andrews McMeel Publishing, 4520 Main Street, Kansas City, Missouri 64111.

*To Lucy*

# My Life As a Dog

I greet.

I inspect.

I kvetch.

I cower.

I tower.

I spar.

I surrender.

I hurt.

I flirt.

I climb.

I canoe.

I drive.

I tour.

I tire.

I frolic.

I chew.

I rue.

I smile.

I cry.

I shake.

I bake.

I play.

I protect.

I spy.

I fly.

I comply.

I sniff.

I wish.

I blush.

I bully.

I prize.

I relish.

I want in.

I wonder.

I ponder.

I snoop.

I snack.

I swab.

I shiver.

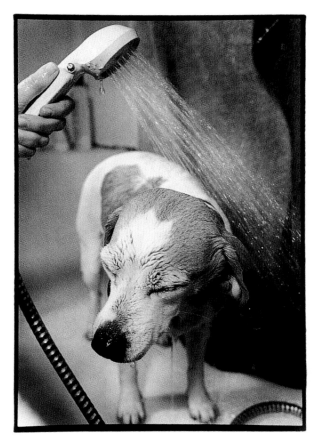

I vamp.

I vent.

I muse.

I preen.

I dream.

I say good-bye.